From My Eyes

Anthony Blakey

authorHOUSE

AuthorHouse™
1663 Liberty Drive, Suite 200
Bloomington, IN 47403
www.authorhouse.com
Phone: 1-800-839-8640

© 2008 Anthony Blakey. All rights reserved.

No part of this book may be reproduced, stored in a retrieval system, or transmitted by any means without the written permission of the author.

First published by AuthorHouse 10/1/2008

ISBN: 978-1-4389-2282-9 (sc)

Printed in the United States of America
Bloomington, Indiana

This book is printed on acid-free paper.

Dedication

To "Momma and Daddy", Thank you for showing me what true love signify.

Momma, thank you for your inspiration. Thank s for "always" relying on God for everything. For this, I will always know where my strength comes from.

Daddy, thank you for humor. Thanks for showing me that nothing can stress us. Nothing! From You is where I get my calm spirit.

To the strongest man and woman I have ever known......

I Love You

Acknowledgements and Special Thanks

To my Son, You are the reason I am here. I love you.

To my sisters, thanks for giving me a woman's point of view. Thanks for your support, guidance and love. I needed it.

To my brothers, (my camp) thanks for the support. Our strength comes in our numbers. No one can stop us now. No one!

To my True friends, I can't thank you all enough. Thanks for the encouragement and support. You all are in my heart. I will never forget all of you.

Lastly, to the love of my life, words could never express my gratefulness. Thank you for the years and the new experiences every day. You are the reason why I write.

Contents

It Feels like November	1
Can I Have You?	2
Almond Kiss	4
Until You Return	6
Wake Up	8
A Long Walk	10
Kiss The Wind	11
Release	12
I Feel For You	14
Love Made Us	16
Out	18
Black Love	19
Please Don't Leave…..	20
In Between Thoughts	21
Melanie's Request	22
WALK WITH ME	23
(My Friend)	24
Chase the Clouds	25
Invisible Heart	26
Scott Messer	27
REPLICA (My Son)	28
Permission	30
A Place	31
Undeserved Love	32
Blank Thoughts	34
How can I ever Thank You?	35
Love Evolution	36
Can I get it back	38
Chances	40
On my heart's side	41

With Empty hands	42
Hug Me	44
What is…	46
Today	47
Beauty	48
Sentence Me	50
Our Secret	52
Epidemic	53
Why Me?	54
Foolish	56
It's Said	58
Betrayal	59
Does He	60
Let Me Sleep	62
Be Honest	64
Silent	65
Puzzle Piece	66
Let's Talk	68
The Essence of You and I	69
Let it Be…	70
I will Miss Tomorrow	72
Lord How Can I…	73

It Feels like November

It feels like November.

When the wind blows,

It's altered from the humid summer air to a swift brisk breeze.

When the gray fluffy clouds cover the sky,

And the blue jays flock together and fly west.

Do your feelings change with the four seasons?

Are you well grounded in Us?

My limbs are bare,

And my orange and red autumn leaves have blows across the fields

I'm lost without your Love…….

Can I Have You?

Our first meeting was magnificent and everything flowed well.

The evening was indescribable.

If I could control time, I would freeze that moment.

I could live for that Saturday night again and again.

Is it I? Or do you feel this power too?

I know our introduction is still fresh.

Are you feeling me like I'm feeling you?

Questions are rumbling in my thoughts.

Why are you looking at me this way?

Your eyes calling my name,

As you turn to hide shared emotions.

These actions are synchronized.

All I want to do is please you,

To love you with the energy God gives me,

These are not just words,

My heart is quietly screaming out.

Can you hear it?

I whisper, sweet nothings in your ear,

Like a pitcher to a glass, my tongue is to your ear,

I transfer my soul to yours.

I hope you open your heart to me,

You're all that I have ever dreamed a real woman to be,

My life is on pause until you take it off,

My mama said that I'd know when true love bit me

And your sting is bittersweet,

With you, I'm complete.

I don't mean to ramble or even repeat my emotions

Just one more minute, and one last question

Can I have you?

Almond Kiss

You will never know who you really are.

For you are unlike any other.

Unfamiliar and unappreciated to most.

I've studied you and your ways

You've stretched me your hand and when I touched you,

I felt Heaven.

In your eyes there is a glass hallway that channels back to the "Garden of Eden".

If you gaze long enough, you'll see the lilies and roses that blossom there.

Take me there.

Your friendship is unique to me.

Without resistance my heart allows me to confide in your soul.

Calm you are.

I just yearn for one long dance with you.

Then I can pronounce that I've danced with God's only daughter.

Your spirit is not of this earth, but heaven sent.

Your smile is innocent.

Your lips are soft and smooth like a pillar of silk raindrops.

Can I have my almond kiss?

Until You Return

Seated comfortably on the hallway floor,

I lounge and inhale the scented air you left.

Rolling the tennis ball back and forth

Against the hardwood that is beneath me

I think of you.

Slowly drifting away in our own existence.

I meditate on all of your precious characteristics

And it quietly takes my breath away.

From your silky smooth skin, to your gentle touch.

From your sweet soft lips

To the glisten in your eyes,

I'm with you again…

At that moment my soul releases a thankful sigh.

Our lovemaking is on repeat in my mind.

Feeling you close to me

Grasping the perfect curve of your back

I paint kisses on your neck.

I can feel your soul talking back to me.

I feel your arms pulling me deeper in,

You put me in a Lover's Coma,

I rest there,

You abide with me there,

I wait there,

Until you return (to me).

Wake Up

Like a rose that blooms in the middle of spring,

Your red apple color pedals were full of charisma and vigor.

Your stems were proud and adequately rooted.

The world would yearn to watch you in amazement as they passed by your garden.

Yet Contentment desired you…

He grew himself beside you..

With each season to transpire, he began to also flourish and rot.

As his branches enhanced,

it commenced to entangle and uproot Life from You.

You touched the forbidden fruit.

Chaos was in your appetite….

Have the Angels turned their backs to you?

Has your Garden now become Desolate?

As you sleep in this Coma,

Your dry red pedals slowly float down to the Earth.

My eye's grieve upon your appearance….

Here is my hand,

Wake up and reach out for life.

With a fresh breath, attain your strength back.

A Long Walk

Let me take your thoughts for a walk

In the day,

When the sky is covered with gray pillow like clouds.

Where we can run freely in the corn fields like five year old children.

Where the blue tinted grass is waist-high

Playing together never to get weary.

Let me take your thoughts for a walk…

In the night,

Where only the light comes from the stars and the yellow lit moon

Where our hands are closely clamped and our fingertips are entangled as we walk across the beach.

The salty ocean will rinse away the grains of sand from our feet

As we just talk.

Come walk with me.

Kiss The Wind

Sitting at my bedside

I gaze at the trees as their leaves are blown afar,

I'm missing you…

I understand that I am far away from you.

But my heart wants only to beat at your rhythm

Being with you makes me complete.

Can I blow in the wind?

Like the leaves that move from one piece of the earth to another.

This is my purpose.

Whenever you think of me

Or need my embrace,

The ground will slowly rotate,

The air will lift me,

Bringing me closer to you.

When you close your eyes

And feel the wind on your face

Kiss me back…

Release

I heard a voice that left a stain on my cerebellum

Who is this on my line?

This voice is familiar

I know it very well.

I remember it.

Queen right?

You've came to me before, in my subconscious.

Tall, Seductive, and Exotic..

The visionary of you was blurry, yet I saw your silhouette.

Your warm hands grasped my dreads

As I knelt down between your knees and thighs.

Your eyes rolling to the back of your brain.

You moaned as you saw the sweat beading down my spine.

Each one of my dreads entangled between your fingers and palm.

Tighter and tighter your grip enhances

As you thrive to hold back what's natural.

"Let it go and be free!" is what's whispered in your ears, though I haven't moved.

This Queen can't explain how she sees me naturally below her, yet behind her at the same time.

She shakes her head from side to side with great force,

As though she wants to wake up from this dream…

I clutch her there.

She can't escape this dream.

She mutters as she knows there is no exit.

Finally be free! (her insides scream out)

Shaking with tears in her eyes

She releases her Honey.

I Feel For You

Rotating many positions through the night

I know that you are there.

Sleeping silently,

I remember holding you.

Pasted together as if we were the wind and air,

When you breathe, I breathe

As if we share the same lungs.

As metal is to a magnet,

I sustain you…

Unbreakable is what we are.

Gently resting your head upon my bare chest,

I watch over you.

Any hint that your soul is uncomfortable,

I will adjust.

I'll alter myself,

So your mind and body stays at rest.

Ravishing you are,

Your beauty speaks for itself,

Without saying any words.

When you are exhausted and your soul is weary,

Come to me….I will feel for you.

Love Made Us

Our bodies cemented together like a brick,

Woven and twisted together like the symbol of infinity.

This has got to be a dream!

Is it?

If so, I must awake at any moment

Sweat is starting to bead up all over us.

The motion of back and forth begins to harmonize

With every stroke there is a soft and subtle moan

Clamped together,

It seems as nothing can separate us,

Being inside her,

I not only feel her but I can feel my inner heartbeat

I notice that our hearts are beating

To the same rhythm

Kissing, touching, tasting

And our hands are still tightly gripped,

Everything in this moment is perfect.

She is perfect!

Is this love?

Did we make love?

I think…

LOVE made us.

Out

She must have misunderstood it.

My love is uncommon to the average.

My emotions do not fluctuate and my affection is consistent.

It does not dissolve away like a puddle of rain that stares at the sun.

What was her boundary?

Where did I tread over her border line?

At what point did I misinterpret her happiness?

I gave my inner soul for years!

Years that added to decades, but now she wants out?

Out, like the foggy steam that departs from my cup of coffee.

"Out!" she articulates, as she strides out of the Starbucks.

Black Love

Have you ever been embraced by one of us?

A real Black Man?

We are true.

We love like no other.

We care like no other

We touch and taste like no other.

We are built like no other.

We are God fearing like no other.

A True Black Man will leave you without any worries.

We are strong enough to rise up against anyone who tries to disrespect you and yours.

We are caring enough to stoke every vessel that you were given.

We are sensitive enough to even understand pillow talk.

We are educated enough to indulge in the most intellectual dialog.

We are spiritual enough to follow God, and lead a family.

If you haven't been blessed by true "Black Love", I pray that Love like ours seek and finds you .

Please Don't Leave…..

I can't imagine my life without you..

We had our problems and disagreements in the past,

Yet we are still here.

I believe God put you in my life for a reason, but what is it?

All I know is that I can't and won't let us go.

I miss you.

I miss our good times and I miss holding you.

However, I see the love in your eyes starting to gloss over.

Now they are pale stares.

Do you still want us?

Have you prayed for something or someone new?

Are our problems a sign from heaven leading us apart?

If we fight to make it work are we resisting God's will?

Has our season come to an end?

In Between Thoughts

We were the combo that was unpronounced.

The dual punch that is unstoppable.

Where are you now?

I sometimes yearn for your spirit.

We've both grown apart and galloped down separate valleys.

Our strength together was supposed to be eternal.

That was our vow.

Your voice is still unforgettable.

Your tone could sing out to the heavens and make the Angels dance a slow grove.

"Sing my love, sing!" is what I chanted nightly.

All of these memories I've secretly kept away in my treasure chest.

Come and let me find you Song bird,

I yearn for your melody..

I will never forget what we shared, as I lay here in between thoughts.

Melanie's Request

This gorgeous red bone sat at my table, just her and I.

At a glance, you would have imagined that she was the center of conversations as everyone looked upon her.

Her eyes were caramel brown and her eye liner was black as midnight.

Her cheeks bones were strong with a sharp smooth smile.

Bright white teeth and a silky pink tongue in which her words just flowed.

The vibe she displayed, were one in which had strength that couldn't be cracked.

Beautiful, Cocky, and Determined.

Determined to let anyone who approached her fence to, "beware of dog"

I couldn't comprehend why she was so unbreakable.

Hard as if cement had just settled over her heart and dried out for days.

She stared at me and asked if I could "shock and amaze" her.

As if she had been on this planet before and there was nothing that she hasn't experienced from the male species.

I leaned towards her and whispered a few words into her ear…

I then kissed her cheek, walked away and watched while a tear rolled down onto her faint smile.

Walk With Me

Walk with me (will you)

Hold my hand as we breathe in the scent of the oceans' tide.

With the soft summer wind in our face,

Tell me who you are.

For I know the exterior of your image,

But reveal to me your interior.

Let's talk about your most sentiment secrets and I share with you mine.

Our trust and bond can never be broken.

Depend on me.

As though I am your spine that allows you to walk upright.

I want you to see beyond my past and view me as I am.

Your True Friend.

A word that is secrete when you utter it from your lips.

We shall go beyond all limits in this relationship.

You are special to me and for that I will never loosen this grip.

(My Friend)

Sometimes my feelings cannot be written down onto paper.

Breathless and lost for words,

You are my all.

Everything!-that is what you mean to me.

You made me a believer of us.

I never truly had a Friend.

Only my family, because they are a part of me.

You enlightened me of another side.

With honesty and loyalty you've established our foundation.

Nothing can untangle this knot that we share.

Forever bonded with God's hand and sealed with Heaven's Stamp.

I will forever Love You

You are my Friend….

Chase the Clouds

Can we drift away silently?

Leaving tomorrow, never to return…

Traveling to places that our eyes have never rested upon.

Can we stay afloat?

Moving swiftly as we chase the clouds..

Let's follow them and go where they go…

Where do these fluffy clouds sleep?

Do they rest?

Do they take pride in floating across the sky, and seeing every bit of the Earth….

Take my hand and go with me?

Invisible Heart

If my heart was invisible

How would you be able hurt me?

You can't touch and damage what you can't see…

My heart is not on display,

So that you're tainted hands could grasp my emotions to use it for toiling.

If my heart was invisible

My soul would be shielded.

Protected by the guardians sent from Heaven,

Only to allow true Love that is sacred to abide in my heart's presence.

So, Love…

Please open your eyes and see me….

Scott Messer

Stand still Scott..

See what is all around you.

You are there now,

You are in God's inner court.

Paradise is in your grasp.

Celebrate for eternity Scott, you made it.

Our minds can't fathom why you were chosen.

Hand picked by God to come home.

Iraq was your fate.

Fighting for a cause that YOU believed in.

No matter the reason, you walked that road,

Head high and chest out without hesitation.

I admire that!

Vick's little brother had grown up to become a man, now a Hero.

We will miss you Scott.

Save me a seat, I'll be there soon.

Until then, we will remember you.

Stand still Scott…

See what is all around you, for you are seeing Heaven!

"3/06"

*R*EPLICA *(My Son)*

As I am of my father

You are of me.

Pure replica.

From the eyes of my eyes

To the blood of my veins

We are the same.

Like a tree, you are apart of me

Stemming away like a branch,

We are from the same roots.

You can depend on me.

No matter how far out your limbs may reach

Know that I am well rooted to Endure, Hold, and Support you.

Permission

I can't sing you an opera

But my love for you allows me to write a melody.

A voice that can't speak

But with love that's shown like sound language for the hearing impaired.

Allow me to be who I am without deception.

Allow me to give all that I have to you without hesitation.

Just allow me

A Place

Is there such a place?

A place where I am engraved with your closeness,

Where we can slow dance in the Garden of Eden.

A place where we lay and just softly whisper lullabies to one another.

Where I can enjoy hearing your faint melancholy tone voice.

A place where you and I are the only creators that roam this universe joyfully.

Where we just depend on one another.

A place where we will live and grow old together

In that world,

After our deaths we still abide amongst each other..

Take me to that place.

Undeserved Love

Concentrating on your essence

I sit here and ponder,

A woman of your stature is difficult to come by.

To even call you my woman is sacred

Why did you even give me a chance?

A man like me could not be worthy of your time.

Clean as December snowflakes

And pure as a virgin's blood,

You are flawless.

Because I've been blessed to have you,

It will be my obligation to worship you.

Not that you are a God, but you are God-sent.

Cherishing every second that the clock hand turns,

I will love you.

My words,

Nor any poem that I utter

can show my real feelings for you.

I will be eternally grateful because you love me.

Every breath that I inhale,

Will I commit toward your every yearning.

When the day comes

when I am laid to rest,

And my eyes are ever more to be closed,

Even then,

Know that I am forever yours.

Blank Thoughts

Thoughts racing.

Heart beat thumping uncontrollably.

I feel the temperature increases as all the stares across this room looks upon me.

The palm of my hand is damp with moisture from perspiration.

"Keep your composure" I think to myself

From my bent knee,

I raise my head.

Looking into her eyes I find myself lost.

Her skin is clear, smooth, and soft.

She holds a smile that can't be mimicked or duplicated.

With a touch of a angles' wing

I Love her.

She is my Queen, Companion, and Friend.

Pulling myself back to this moment

I watch as she stares off into my pupils.

Will you let me Love you now and forever?
Will you marry me?

How can I ever Thank You?

You watched over me

You showed me right from wrong

You've always set a good example

There isn't any other greater image of parents than you too..

You shared with me your wisdom, knowledge, and were so understanding.

You never broke promises because your word was your bond.

I praise God with every breath for sending you into my life.

You've supported me through my good and bad decisions.

You've celebrated with me my joys and embraced me through my tears

God has truly opened his window and shined his light upon your face.

I only pray that I can be just like you

Faithful you have been.

And for that I will always Love the God that is in you.

There is no way I could even express my appreciation in words

I will remember this always….

I Love You Both Mom and Dad…

Love Evolution

If my life was the universe,

She would be my galaxy.

Her love for me keeps me leveled,

As gravity keeps me grounded.

The brief moment we met,

Was as swift as Haley's Comet flashing across the sky.

She makes my world spin on its axle,

When I'm stressed and frustrated,

She calms and covers me.

Like an eclipse,

She is beautiful.

All the stars shine through her eyes.

She is my sun and moon.

She awakes me every morning with her love,

As the sun peaks through my window.

At night I quietly and peacefully rest,

Because I know the Heavens are watching over us.

Was our love predestined?

Was our meeting inevitable?

Love at first sight?

Or can this love be considered…

Our "BIG BANG THEORY?"

Where Love's Evolution began.

Can I get it back

You were my life, love, and my purpose.

She was meant for my everyday living.

I had a good thing at the wrong time,

and yet it slipped through my hands.

Trying to keep her was like trying to hold a fist full of sand all day.

With every movement, a grain of the sand slithers through my fingers and knuckles.

I tried loving with everything.

Everything!

Her heart was full and glowed every time I entered her presents.

Yet my heart was half full.

I want to glow like she does.

I want to smile with the same excitement that she has.

Can I get it back?

There was a time when I could smell her aroma two blocks away.

I could anticipate her taste buds desires and have the equivalent yearning.

How did this alter?

How did you maintain the same dedication to us?

Where have I mistaken? What shift in my heart did I construct?

I demand that my heart beats back to its original rhythm.

I need to love you completely before all of this sand has left my fist…..

Chances

If this is the other side,

Why isn't the grass green?

Could this be how my dices have been rolled?

I took a chance on love and lust

Yet I am empty

I could have stayed.

I should have stayed!

I thought that someone else could hold me tighter.

I thought that someone else could make me laugh longer.

I thought that someone else could love me better.

Oh but how incorrect was I.

Each day that I awake, I am reminded of this lesson.

On my heart's side

Stand close to me my princess

I offer you these Persian roses.

You are the reason why God breathes on the earth and the winds blows.

He wants the universe to inhale your aroma

Your love is much sweeter than the spring honeysuckle.

Stand close to me my princess

It's ok to weep.

Life can sometimes compress us.

As though we have vice grips around the waist.

Hold on to me, my love

I'll never bend or break.

Rest your head on my chest.

On the side where my heart beats constantly,

That's the home for my love.

With Empty hands

Born with just a family and a last name

I have nothing.

No fame or fortune.

No excessive amount of cash flow.

Yet, what I do have is my empty hands stretched to the sky.

"Give it to me", I yell out to the heavens

"Give me what I deserve!"

Waiting for an answer or a reason to go on,

I obtain nothing but a thought.

A deliberation,

No!..a passion rebirth within me to write.

Write and give the world my song.

My song that will be heard from corner to corner across the globe.

Hear my song for it will play throughout eternity

I will write this song with nothing more than my "empty hands"…..

Hug Me

The previous day has come and gone

And I needed you to hug me.

I awake today to the dog barking,

Wanting to be taken out side.

We stare at one another as we brush our teeth over our matching "his and her" sink. (smiling at me)

You quickly press my shirt while I pack my lunch.

I adore you.

Rushing out the door headed to work I yell out " I'm gone.. Love you!"

Work and more work piles up at my cubical

"This crap sucks", I think out loud.

Deadlines and conference calls distract me from dreaming of you.

Just to make it until 5pm is everyone's prayer.

My lunch break gets shorter and shorter each day of the year.

Now back to the rat race.

Call after call my neck begins to ache.

At last, 5pm arrives.

You would assume that we're all derby horses that just got released from the gates as we stamped to the parking lot.

Finally I exhale as I drive home.

I pull up to you at the door ready to greet me.

The day has come and gone.

I drop the brief case as you reach out to Hug Me.

What is...

What is better than a Rose?

Is there anything?

Something that is so appealing to the eye and delicate to your nose.

It's tender and sensitive.

Something that everyone yearns to hold next to their heart.

What is better than a Summer Breeze?

A breeze that is unruffled to the skin and embraces your soul.

What is better than spring rain?

Soft mystic tear drops that when it falls from the sky it can tattoo you from head to toe.

What is better than the thought of being in heaven?

A kingdom in which every soul desires to dwell.

A place to love and be loved

What is better?

My Love, you are....

Today

This has got to be one of the best days of my life.

Today I feel as if I am next to God's window and I can see within.

Have you ever felt that way?

As if troubles were many miles from your exit.

Not only are all my problems now a blear in the fog, but I have a woman that I see so clear to me

To have been held with her love and the support of the heavens….

This is unutterable.

Beauty

She has a queen's image,

The kind that forces you to wonder off into the future.

With the beauty of a rainbow,

The strength of an ox,

The charisma of a statue that stares back,

There is no better sight.

Just a glimpse of her silhouette,

And you'll daydream all day.

At birth it was obvious that she was meant for royalty,

Her words are powerful.

A touch from her,

And your body becomes paralyzed and relaxed.

Her whisper will put you in a coma,

And a smile from her face will make your being start to glow.

To me,

She is everything

I am the thunder,

She is my lightening,

She is my heart, my hope, and my dream

My way is never dark,

Cause she's my Divya.

*Divya = (Light in the temple)

Sentence Me

Some say it's a sin to love the way that I do
But that's only because they don't have you.
I awake with my diamond every morning
And lay down at night with my dreams beside me.
I'd swear to any courtroom, before any judge,
That I'm guilty of only one crime.
That's being in love your Honor.
Can you tell?
Don't you see the gleam in my eyes?
Nothing else matters, for her I'd do anything.
So charge me if you must, I won't put up a fuss.
If you take away my freedom, it will be okay
Because I still have a piece of her heart
And she'd still have me always.

Lock me up but you can never arrest fate.

I was born to adore her and made to make her happy.

My soul claps for her, so carefully deliberate

Don't falsely accuse

Use all the facts

But know this, if I had it all to do again,

I'd love her just the same.

I'm prepared to serve my time.

No matter what happens, you can't separate us

Or kill the love we share inside

Cause it's stronger than pride

She's my mountain in any valley

My treasure divine, more than semi-precious

My diamond in the rough,

She is the best thing to me that has ever happened

So again, sentence me if you must.

Our Secret

I know you are real.

Now I can see.

I have seen wonders that only you can perform

I tested you, and with your mercy you have shown me the way.

I used to think that my life situations and trials were just random occurrences.

Yet you have revealed to me differently.

Thank you for letting me feel your presence and showing me your face.

I will never doubt you again.

Epidemic

Being in love can sometimes kill you in your sleep
Studying her beauty from afar,
She can be a virus eating well into the deep.

Deep until she is well rooted in your soul,
Things start to happen,
You can't understand it and you lose control.

She is like a contagious yearning,
Seeking to touch your innermost desires,
Sometimes I wonder,
Is it her warmth or the beauty of her blaze,
That leads me to her fire.

I fan her…
With my thoughts, memories and reflections,
Yet her appearance is just a deception.

One kiss,
And she has you hooked,
You think you're special
But to her,
You're just another chapter in her diary book.

Why Me?

Why me God?

Am I chosen for a reason?

As if you were strolling deep in the valleys and through gravel and shrubs you stumbled upon me.

Why am I here?

Trying to untangle my own life isn't that simple.

Speak out to me my purpose!

Or just whisper it to me.

Must I assume my destiny?

With uncertainty, I frequently make mistakes because my foot is unsure of my path.

Then I cause you pain and can no longer feel you.

So I am back to where I started.

Nowhere and alone!

Speak to me, like you spoke to Moses.

Show me the way.

If not, will you answer this.

"Why Me?"

Foolish

Laying down on my bed

I think and really start to see

That through my hard-headedness

You were loyal and a true companion to me.

You took care of me

And you treated me good,

When my family couldn't be there,

Right by my side is where you stood.

For me,

You would give up your last dime,

Or if I needed you,

You would never hesitate,

You were there right on time.

I would be so overwhelmed and busy

And time with you I did not spend,

I know it hurt you

But you told me "you'd be there until the end."

Men make mistakes,

Some simple, some big,

Many are unforgivable.

Remember you can't keep neglecting true love

Cause when it's gone,

You must write it off as a lost

And blame yourself for the cost.

It's Said

They say that she is incredible

Flawless in everything that she does

Her personality and charisma unlike any other.

Beautiful?

Yes....

Her aura is colorful like October leaves

A smile that makes your heart flutter and skip a beat

Her eyes can have you sustained, shackled and chained in your steps.

A delicate touch that can even paralyze your soul.

Who is she? You ask..

Just an Angel.

From a stranger's eye, you'd believe that she is just "common"

But when you get to know her,

When you get to laugh with her,

When you get to touch her

It's then revealed…

That real Angel's can be seen…..

Betrayal

Life is only Life

How much tighter are you going to squeeze this rope?

You were my backbone and my support.

I trusted you.

Yet you would smile back with other intentions.

Trust must be just a common word.

And betrayal was your partner.

You've sat and plotted on the fate of others.

Why fool them?

Be true to yourself before you expect to have a friend.

We are all just a breath away from the grave,

So why waste it deception?

Was it worth it to you?

Are you now satisfied?

Does He

Does God speak to the middle class?

I've heard that he's spoken to the wealthy and shared with them visions.

I've heard that he has even whispered to the homeless to encourage them through their unimaginable harsh times.

But what about most of us?

The one's who barely have enough to make it pay check to pay check.

The one's that depend on a Company rise every January.

The one's that take a deep breath when it's time to take their kids school shopping in the fall.

The one's that pray for a Christmas bonus at the end of the year and hope that their vacation time will roll over to the next year.

The one's that has to consider co-pays into their monthly budget.

The one's that hope their medical insurance doesn't max out, and their auto insurance doesn't lapse.

The one's that contemplate driving off at the pump, because the gas prices have reached 5 dollars a gallon.

The one's that noticed that the price of milk and eggs has gone up almost 2 dollars.

The one's that believe in doing the right thing, however Karma just hasn't come back around the corner to reward them.

What about all of them?

Can you tell me?

Does God speak to the middle class?......

Let Me Sleep

Let me sleep

Because when I'm asleep, I'm away from reality.

When I'm asleep, beauty is in my company

She and I can walk from California to Egypt in seconds

In that moment, we see everything

As if time didn't matter

Because time doesn't exist,

We hold hands because we are one.

Let me sleep,

Because when I'm asleep, I see beauty as she is.

She is into my spirit as I am into her veins,

No tricks, games or gimmicks will be played.

Her honesty is pure,

Pure as fresh water that flows from a mountaintop to the river bed below.

Innocent she is, Innocent as a newborn.

Let me sleep,

Because when I'm asleep, all of my fantasy is fulfilled.

Both my mind and soul yearns for her presence,

I crave only for her scent and her touch.

If you happen to catch me in my resting state

My only request is to please…

"Let Me Sleep."

Be Honest

Can you look in my eyes,

And say what your heart truthfully feels?

Can you tell me what your soul knows?

(To be real)

Don't hold any punches,

Leave the ingredients in.

You can't have the sun without the day.

The moon needs the night.

I believe in you,

I trust your intentions are good

But only you know the truth.

Some people can handle it,

Others cannot

So is a lie really worth it?

The question is…

Can you be honest with yourself?

Silent

Your pain is silent
But my heart can hear its cry
You don't complain.
You even cover up and hide the shame
I see strength in your eyes
And there's power in your smile
Yes!
It's subtle but loud.
I don't ask for much
But my desire is to see you happy.
I would give my all and everything
If that would make your world complete
You are the wheel that moves me
My earth, my sky, even my heart beat.
You don't have to bare this burden alone
I'm here now
On my shoulder you can lean and feel comfort.
My hands will arrest each teardrop as they fall
On me you can depend
In us you can believe
Just talk to me
Baby please
You don't have to be silent anymore.
Not with me…

Puzzle Piece

Though I can't play cards or games in general,
I always finish what I start
And puzzles have always been a challenge to me.

My life is like a puzzle
I desire only to see the picture in its full completion.
Constantly putting pieces together
My life starts to take shape.

With love, I admit
I could never find the right puzzle piece
In and out of relationships,
Trying to make them work
But none of those pieces seemed to fit.

After many attempts, I sit in confusion,

Unsure of my options a prayer must be released above.

Standing still for guidance, he reveals to me one piece standing alone.

Unaccompanied as if it was there all the while waiting for me to seek for it.

With a changed face

I put the piece in.

Now my picture is clear.

Could you be my missing piece?

The piece that I've longed for?

Let's Talk

Let's talk, You and me only

Where can I start?

I'm Tired.

Is there a bigger picture?

Life can seem unreal.

I'm dehydrated from life's deserted and dry promises.

I put my trust in thee, but sometimes I know you are testing me.

How many tests must I pass?

I could feel your presence and essence just last week.

Now, am I on an island?

Deserted? Why? For what?

I was enjoying everything,

Our conversations, and to be able to just abide in you.

There I felt secure.

Nothing mattered.

People, jobs, and life all were just temporary.

Today, life has me in its hands and I worry...

Will I fecl you back tomorrow?

The Essence of You and I

Like a professor,

You have taught me how Love really is

To accept and offer intimacy.

Like a heart surgeon,

The palm of your hands grasps my heart with the most delicate touch

Gentle, baby Gentle

Innocent eyes of a new born infant,

A smile that is blameless,

And all your features are angelic

Has God allowed you to accompany me?

Just talk to me

And watch over me while I rest in your obis....

Let it Be...

Listen while I tell you a point of view.

It can and it will be in time.

I've heard your cry through your MySpace

While other lame nigga's just want to get in your space.

I'm not like them, though you can't tell that through the color of my skin.

Black as midnight, smooth as caramel, hard as a frozen pot pie.

Try me.

Defrost me and know that I provide every vitamin and mineral that your Greek eyes need.

I'm told that you can't mix with co-works because you can't shit where you eat,

But what happens when this "unknown" substance has a hook in me?

Like a butcher that just stuck his sharp blades in my steak.

I could just walk away, however I don't desire that.

I want to be captured.

To capture me would be like to sustain a Unicorn.

Oh yes, they do exist, because I'm right here.

Grazing in your pasture.

Do what you want with me!

Ride me?

Show me off to the local neighbors?

Put your prize on display?

Either will be ok, as long as I'm here to dwell in your aura, I'm content.

Can it happen?

Will it happen?

Most will disagree with the percent of success.

However I'll definitely take that bet.

I will Miss Tomorrow

I will miss tomorrow.

Yet tomorrow is not here

Even though we decided that it's best

That our path is to be separate.

Is that really best?

If so, tomorrow I will let you go,

Only to open my door, allowing Loneliness in to accompany me.

But tonight as we lay one last night and sleep

I will search for a dream.

A dream that comforts all hurt and pain

A dream that sketches your imagine into my memory

While I dream, I pray for a dream to descend upon you

A dream that cruises you down the road of our past happiness

Never to stop.

Slowing down only to take you through each moment of our joy and laughter.

When you awake, will you remember the dream? (And stay?)

*L*ord How Can I...

How can I be like you?

To walk in your image...

For man to look at me and see your presences.

How can I be close to you?

Close enough to where I can feel your embrace when I feel alone.

For you lift my head when I feel that I have failed you.

To know that you are with me through all things.

How can I please you?

For you to look upon me and be proud of your son.

To know that I only live my life to walk in your footsteps

How can I build my Faith?

To really know that you will never leave me

To walk and breathe easily because you are on my side.

Not to have a single worry in the world

Lord how can I?

How many times?

Made in the USA
Lexington, KY
12 June 2017